Be Anxious for Nothing

ARISE

Take Control of Your Soul

Nancy Fraser

Be Anxious for Nothing: ARISE, Take Control of Your Soul

Copyright ©2021 Nancy Fraser

ALL RIGHTS RESERVED. This book contains material protected under International and Federal Copyright Laws and Treaties. Any unauthorized reprint or use of this material is prohibited. No part of this book may be reproduced or transmitted in any form or by any means, electronic or mechanical, including photocopying, recording, or by any information storage and retrieval system without express written permission from the author.

Table of Contents

Introduction 1

Chapter 1: The True You 5

Chapter 2: The Five-Sense Realm 9

Chapter 3: The Relationship 13

Chapter 4: Taking Possession 17

Chapter 5: Fear Not 25

Chapter 6: Living By Faith 29

Chapter 7: The Garden 37

Introduction

MANY ARE SEARCHING FOR self help books to find what they need to deal with anxiety, fear, depression, oppression, and anger. While some of these books may help to a degree, most times it is just putting a band aid on the surface. This can make one feel better for a time but it is far more productive to get to the root of a matter.

This book was written to be a help in understanding that we can take control of our lives through learning the root causes of our challenges. This is a different approach to the mainstream way of dealing with these issues.

I believe that if you read this with an open heart you will see how you can take authority over your soul through your spirit and be made free from the chains that try to bind you.

The realm in which we live is not just what we see, hear, taste, touch and smell. That is what we know as the five-sense realm. There is a spiritual realm which is very present in all of our lives whether we believe it or not.

In the book of Luke chapter 10, Jesus is welcomed into Martha's house but she is distracted with much serving. She starts complaining to Jesus that her sister Mary, who is just sitting and listening to Jesus speak, was not helping her. Jesus told Martha that she was worried and troubled about many things **but one thing is needed** and Mary has chosen that good part which will not be taken away.

Feeding your spirit with God's Word will enable you to be an overcomer of negative circumstances.

The life of victory lies within the ability to enable our spirit to arise on the inside and take control of our soul. My prayer is that you will gain that knowledge and put it into practice for your own life.

Arise
from the depression and prostration
in which circumstances have kept you—
rise to a new life!
Shine (be radiant with the glory of the Lord),
for your light has come,
and the glory of the Lord has risen upon you.
ISAIAH **60:1 (AMP)**

Chapter 1

The True You

THERE IS A PATH TO VICTORY over every circumstance that comes our way, but we must first understand who we are.

SPIRIT, SOUL & BODY

I was in the fitness field for many years and their motto is body, soul and spirit. Always emphasizing the body first the soul second and the spirit last.

That is completely opposite of the way God made us. Believing this way will hinder us from reaching our full potential. It keeps us in a state of mind that we are just a physical body with a soul and a spirit.

This type of thinking makes us body and soul conscious and barely even recognizing that we are a spirit.

NOTICE HOW THE WORD OF GOD DESCRIBES US...

> Now may the God of peace Himself sanctify you completely; and may your whole **spirit, soul, and body** be preserved blameless at the coming of our Lord Jesus Christ.
> 1 THESSALONIANS 5:23 (NKJV)

As it says in Genesis 1:26-27, God made us in His image and likeness, a three part being. We are a spirit, we have a soul and both our spirit and soul live in a body. Just like we live in a house or apartment. When we move we do not take that house or apartment with us but we do take what's inside.

So when we leave the earth our bodies remain and we take what is inside, which is our spirit and soul.

Our soul consist of our mind, within the mind is a conscience and emotions. There we have a free will where our decisions are made. An emotion is a subjective conscious experience relating to the mental process of perception.

How we perceive something will initiate an emotion.

Your thought pattern fixed on any one thing will cause a feeling to arise and that feeling can cause you to behave

in a certain manor. The decision to react to that feeling is always yours and you can have complete control.

You are the boss of your mind, and you can take authority over it.

For example, if you wake up in the morning and it is windy and rainy you have the choice to either be annoyed that you have to go out in the nasty weather or decide to be grateful that you are free and have the ability to go out. If you think on the negative it can ruin your whole day. But if you think on the positive it will set your day on a good course.

As Vivian Greene said...

> "Life isn't about waiting for the storm to pass...
> It's about learning to dance in the rain."

However you choose to forecast the circumstances of life so shall the climate be.

Emotions are within our soul realm and they were given to us by God. As you recall in Genesis, He made us in His image and likeness.

He also has emotions as you can see in the gospels when they speak about how Jesus cried when He heard Lazarus was dead.

In His humanity *Jesus wept* for *Lazarus*; in His divinity He raised him from the *dead.*

Jesus was moved with compassion because He loved the people.

Then there was the time in the garden when He was so stressed about being separated from His heavenly Father before He was to be crucified that He sweat droplets of blood. It was at that moment where His emotions led Him to plead with the Father to take this cup from Him. But then He allowed His Spirit to rise up and He said **"nevertheless, not as I will, but as You will."**

No matter what emotions Jesus was going through He always allowed the Spirit within Him to arise and take control of His soul.

I am often told that I have great will power. The truth is we all have the same amount of will power. The difference is how we use it. For me it is the Holy Spirit within me that drives me to use it to its full potential. You can have that same power.

God has given us our own will but the Holy Spirit can empower us to make the decisions that would bring victory to every circumstance that comes our way.

Chapter 2

The Five-Sense Realm

MOST OF US WERE BROUGHT UP to rely so much on the natural realm and putting our physical bodies first that we automatically yield our emotions according to that five-sense realm.

That means our emotions so easily change by what we see, hear, taste, touch or smell.

Anyone of us can have our emotions changed right now by looking, listening, touching, tasting or smelling something. Take a look around right now.

Are your emotions influenced by what you see outside of the window? The taste of your drink? The background noise level?

You might not think there is anything wrong with that since it has always been that way. I too use to think that as well, as it was all I knew.

The challenge we face when we are moved by the five-sense realm is that our emotions end up controlling us. This can cause us to make wrong decisions and have wrong actions.

God no doubt gave us emotions, but they were designed to enjoy not to be controlled by. He also gave us the five- sense realm to help us know and establish things for our journey here on earth.

However, our emotions were never intended to direct our lives. Therefore, we must employ our emotions to work properly in the five-sense realm.

When you manage or own a business you employ people and train them to do the work for the prosperity of that business. In the same way we must employ and **train our emotions to work for the prosperity of our souls.**

3 John 1:2 (NKJV) says…

> Beloved I pray that you may prosper in all things and be in health **even as your soul prospers.**

This shows the importance of our soul prospering as it is vital not only to our success in life but also to our health and well-being.

If we allow our emotions to be moved by the five-sense realm it will be easy for them to control our thoughts which will control our actions. This can cause us to live a very devastated life. Constantly being moved in and out of our thought patterns. Whether it is getting angry, sad, depressed, offended, fearful or so on. One minute you are happy the next minute you are sad. One minute you are angry the next you are at peace.

The result being an emotional roller coaster hoping you don't fall off the tracks.

Every day we each have a choice to either yield our emotions to the five-sense realm or to the spirit realm. Jesus lived his life as an example. He yielded His emotions to the spirit realm in which empowered Him to have total control over every circumstance. This practice enabled Him to hear from His Heavenly Father and take the right actions.

While we will all go through circumstances in this life that will change our emotions, we should never allow our emotions to change us.

Chapter 3

The Relationship

IN ORDER FOR US TO YIELD our emotions to the spirit realm we need to understand the spiritual relationship we were created for.

I grew up in a denominational church and I am grateful that I was not born in another country or denomination where they did not acknowledge Jesus as God. However, throughout the years of schooling and growing up it was a list of rules, regulations, and religious traditions.

I knew of God but I did not really know Him.

It was not until I accepted the gift of salvation by truly believing in my heart and speaking out of my mouth that Jesus died for my sins and rose again. It was then that I was able to establish a true spiritual relationship with Him.

We have all been separated from God by sin and it is only through acknowledging that Jesus shed His blood for our sins and accepting Him as our Savior that we can be reconciled with God the Father.

> But your iniquities have separated you from your God;
> And your sins have hidden His face from you,
> So that He will not hear...
> **Isaiah 59:2 (NKJV)**

If you haven't done so already you can be reconciled with God by saying this prayer:

> Lord Jesus I believe you died for my sins and rose again to heaven. I ask you to forgive me and I accept you as my Lord and Savior. Thank you Father for sending your Son to pay my debt. Empower me with your Holy Spirit so I can fulfill the life you have for me.
> Amen

All relationships become stronger as we spend time together and get to know each other more intimately. It is the same with God. As we continue to grow in the knowledge of Jesus, **grace and peace are multiplied** to us and we see that it is far more than a religion.

It is a relationship with a living God who loves us so much.

> Grace and peace be multiplied to you in the knowledge
> of God and of Jesus our Lord...
> **2 PETER 1:2 (NKJV)**

The multiplication of grace and peace that grows in us from knowing Him allows us to live free from fear and anxiety.

Everyone who truly believes in their heart and accepts Jesus as their Lord and Savior **AND** continues to grow in the knowledge of Him will see that it is His life, His Spirit in us, bearing witness with our spirit.

This enables us to be grateful for what He did for us and it will draw us into that close relationship with Him. A relationship where-by we can talk to God just like He is here with us. Gaining the ability to go to Him without fear, receiving everything He has for us. Being able to confidently come boldly to His throne of grace, which is our very present help in times of trouble.

> So let us come boldly to the throne of our gracious
> God. There we will receive His mercy, and we will find
> grace to help us when we need it most.
> **HEBREWS 4:14-16 (NLT)**

This is the freedom to fellowship with Him in joy and peace. Access to a real conversation with God, knowing His goodness and mercy while experiencing His love.

> Enter into **His** gates with thanksgiving,
> And into **His courts** with praise.
> Be thankful to Him, and bless **His** name.
> **Psalm 100:4 (NKJV)**

Jesus is not a task master looking to control our lives and beat us over the head if we make a mistake. He is love and He is full of grace and mercy. He gave us a free will and offered us the choice of life and freedom.

God endeavors to help us by guiding our paths and showing us the best way. But He will never go against the free will He gave us.

> Therefore if the Son makes you free,
> you shall be free indeed.
> **John 8:36 (NKJV)**

Getting to know Him is the key and we do that through spending time learning His Word and talking to Him, thanking Him for all He has done.

> Today I have given you the choice
> between **life** and death, between **blessings** and curses.
> Now I call on heaven and earth to witness the **choice you make. Oh, that you would choose life,**
> so that you and your descendants might live!
> **Deuteronomy 30:19 (NLT)**

Chapter 4

Taking Possession

THE FINAL DECISIONS ARE up to us not Him. We make those decisions through our conscience and if we allow our emotions to be controlled by the five-sense realm we will not make the right decisions in life.

Whatever we don't rule over will rule over us.

There is a phrase we use that says train of thought. The same way a train will take you somewhere if you get on it is the same way a train of thought will take you somewhere if you allow your mind to ride on it. We must control our thoughts to ensure we get on the right train.

Our thought patterns will determine where we go, what we say and what we do.

For example if something in the natural makes you fearful and you get on that train of thought you will react to fear and most likely make the wrong decision. Emotionalism will not only hurt you mentally but it will also hurt you physically and can overtake you spiritually.

Emotional stress is one of the most debilitating things that someone can do to themselves. That person becomes mentally and physically exhausted to the point of manifesting real physical symptoms in their body.

It is important to learn by faith how NOT to yield your emotions to the five-senses and get on the wrong train of thought. We want to control our thought pattern and stay on track to success instead of being derailed to defeat.

Affirmations, meditations and positive thinking is all good and can be a help to people. But in order to take complete control over your soul you must have the Holy Spirit living in you and you must renew your mind with God's Word.

When you receive Jesus as your Savior as I discussed in the previous chapter He gives you His Spirit.

Jesus explained in the book of John in chapters 14 to 16 that the Holy Spirit will lead and guide you into all truth. He (the Holy Spirit) will be a helper and bring things to our remembrance. The Holy Spirit is also called the comforter as He brings us peace.

We were never created to be separated from Him.

In John 14:8 Jesus says He will not leave us orphans but will send His Spirit. That is why there can seem to be a void or loneliness in someones heart no matter how many relationships they have.

In Romans 8:16 it explains that His Holy Spirit bears witness with our hearts that we are now children of God. No longer orphans and alone but now He lives on the inside of us.

Going forward we can live our lives with confidence and courage to not be afraid.

Psalm 23 (NKJV) says...

> Even though we walk through the valley of the shadow of death we will fear no evil for He is with us!

> Jesus said He will never leave us nor forsake us.
> **HEBREWS 13:5 (NKJV)**

So you can see how receiving Him and His Holy Spirit can be critical to your well being.

The Holy Spirit needs to be the foundation of your conscience if you want to posses your soul.

As you allow Him to guide you into all truth through learning the Word of God He will teach you how to live a life of victory.

The popular saying "it is what it is" doesn't have to be a reality in our lives. That is accepting whatever life sends our way.

But as we are instructed in the passage in Romans 4:17 ....God gives life to the dead and calls those things which do not exist as though they did.

It is what we say it is...that can truly be the reality in our lives.

Proverbs 18:21 (NKJV) says...

> Death and Life are in the power of the tongue.

Our words are powerful and can either produce life or death.

The word of God tells us when we accept Jesus as our Saviour we are now reconciled with our heavenly Father and are children of God.

> ... and if children, then **heirs**—
> **heirs** of God and joint **heirs** with Christ.
> **ROMANS 8:17 (NKJV)**

As heirs of His Kingdom it belongs to us and we do have the ability to possess our souls and take control over our emotions. Not allowing them to be moved by the five-sense realm but instead by the Word and Spirit of God. This empowers us to take authority over negative circumstances and trials in our life.

If you were born into a royal family you would have some benefits of being in that royalty. If someone tried to tell you something different or take away what belonged to you either you would disregard what they said knowing how foolish they were or take your authority over what is endeavoring to take something away that belongs to you.

Jesus said…

> "I will give you the keys of the kingdom of heaven; whatever **you** bind on earth will be bound in heaven, and whatever **you** loose on earth will be loosed in heaven."
> MATTHEW 16:19 (NKJV)

This means it is up to us not Him and whatever we choose all the power in heaven backs us up here on earth.

As children of God it is part of who we are and what Jesus deposits in us when we receive His Holy Spirit.

We must never allow what someone does or says to us define who we are. Nor shall we allow them to move us

into an emotional state of despair. Which can come in the form of depression, anger, anxiety or the like.

> For **we** are **not** wrestling with flesh and blood [contending only with physical opponents], but against the despotisms, against the powers, against [the master spirits who are] the world rulers of this present darkness, against the spirit forces of wickedness in the heavenly (supernatural) sphere.
> **EPHESIANS 6:12 (AMP)**

Behind the scenes there is a real spiritual realm of forces that guide others to do what they do. Instead of reacting to the person in a state of emotionalism we act in our spiritual authority. Continuing to walk in peace and love.

There are times we will give love or show mercy to someone, or go out of our way to help them. Then we look for it back from the same person and when we do not see it we get angry or disappointed.

The bible does tell us we reap what we sow but it does not say it will always come from the same place we sowed it. Therefore, do not allow yourself to get discouraged if that same person does not return the gesture. God is faithful and He will bring it another way.

> And let us not grow weary while doing good, for in due season we shall reap if we do not lose heart.
> **GALATIANS 6:9 (NKJV)**

Unforgiveness, bitterness, strife and anger will only hurt us. It is our job to walk in the fruits of the spirit He gave us which is...love, joy, peace, patience, kindness, goodness, faithfulness, gentleness and long-suffering.

Most people put total responsibility on God in the wrong way by blaming Him for everything. There are times He may direct us in a certain way and we do not heed to His voice. Then something may go wrong and we end up blaming Him.

In reality, while God is the Creator and He is Sovereign He gave us a free will. We have the responsibility to fulfill the things He has called us to on earth, but He will never force us, He will only guide us.

When we possess our soul it is like an anchor to our spirit. We are a three part being and in the natural majority rules. The flesh yields to the five senses and if you allow your soul to line up with your flesh it will make decisions according to the five-sense realm.

This is contrary to the way God has made you to be.

When you possess your soul and take control of your emotions, by the Word of God through faith, it will anchor to your spirit. Always upholding your spirit. Then you will make decisions according to your spirit.

As I mentioned before the fruits of the spirit that is given to us as children of God we now have love and patience. When we employ the love and patience given to us, it will bring forth the spiritual power that will hold our soul in perfect balance with our spirit.

> But let patience have its perfect work, that you may be perfect and complete, lacking nothing.
> **JAMES 1:4 (NKJV)**

Chapter 5

Fear Not

IF YOU HAVE NOT ALREADY taken notice there are so many things designed to produce fear. News media and certain commercials are filled with implanting thoughts of fear. Sales commercials or sales in general can use fear tactics to get you to make a purchase. Then there are movies, TV shows and songs that will endeavor to implant fear of all kinds of things.

Before you know it there are constant thoughts of fear which create anxiety that can lead to the point of panic attacks.

Fear is a spirit not an emotion and the Word of God consistently tells us to either fear not, do not be afraid or do not worry.

Fear is caught through exposure and it endeavors to come upon you. We NEED to RESIST it at all costs.

> For God has not given us the spirit of fear
> but of power and of love and a sound mind.
> **2 Timothy 1:7 (NKJV)**

There will be people near and far who will speak words and have actions that will try to move you by the spirit of fear. If allowed, this spirit can create actions of anxiety, depression, anger, pride, bitterness, feelings of unworthiness and so on.

The spirit of fear has the ability to take over your imagination if you allow it to.

Fear will cause you to say and do things that can have a negative impact on your life. It has the ability to make you physically sick.

If you let it take control it will paralyze your forward momentum by implanting panic and anxiety attacks. It has the capacity of draining peace and joy right out of your life.

Just as certain trees and plants thrive in certain climates so shall our souls.

A palm tree will flourish and grow to its fullest potential in warmer more humid climates. It may still live and do well in other climates but it will never grow to its full potential.

In order to not allow the spirit of fear to move you out of the climate of peace and joy you must resist it and take in what the Word of God says.

In Colossians chapter 3 it tells us to **set our mind** on things above not on things of the earth. It also tells us to put off such things as anger, wrath and malice and to put on such things as love, tender mercies and kindness. **It is all a choice and up to us, we are in control.**

That is why we must not put ourselves in a position where fear will be allowed to take root in our lives. Yes, it will come at times but it is up to us to cast it off.

Your imagination does not have a mind of it's own. It will follow whatever you set it on. When you set your mind on the Word of God you will think differently. You will walk with the sound mind He created you to have. Remember, God did not give us the spirit of fear, but power love and a sound mind.

1 John 4:18 (NLT) tells us...

> Such love has no fear,
> because perfect love expels all fear.

If we are afraid, it is for fear of punishment, and this shows that we have not fully experienced His perfect love.

In the Greek language the meaning of expels or another version says casts (as in perfect love "expels or "casts" out fear) a violent displacement.

When you truly know how much God loves you the fear will violently be displaced from your life.

That is why it is of the utmost importance to renew your mind with God's Word.

> My child, pay attention to what I say Listen carefully to my words. Don't lose sight of them Let them penetrate deep into your heart For they are life to those who find them and healing to their whole body.
> **Proverbs 4:20-22 (NLT)**

Gods Word will not only heal your soul but it will heal your physical body.

This will ensure you to live as an overcomer and be victorious over every circumstance that comes your way in life.

> Let not your heart be troubled neither let it be afraid, Believe in God; believe also in me.
> **John 14:1 (NKJV)**

Chapter 6

Living By Faith

WHAT IS FAITH AND HOW do we successfully live by it?

> Now faith means putting our full confidence
> in the things we hope for, it means being certain
> of things we cannot see.
> **HEBREWS 11:1 (PHILLIPS TRANSLATION)**

The hope that is referred to is an expectation. People who have issues with anxiety, depression and anger have an expectation of something negative. If you tell them things will get better their "I hope so" is in a doubting frame of mind. The underlying root of this is some type of fear. Remember in the previous chapter we talked about how fear is not an emotion but it is a spirit. When someone continues to meditate on the negative expectation, that underlying root of fear will take control. Therefore their "doubting" hope is faith in something negative to happen.

When you have an expectation (hope) of something positive your faith in that will come to life and take control. **Hope is the anchor to faith.**

I liken it to being on a boat and whether you are in the bay or the ocean and you stop to fish or relax you must anchor the boat or it will be moved. It doesn't matter how calm the water is, if you do not drop the anchor you will eventually be moved out of the place you stopped. Then if the wind starts blowing or another boat comes by and rocks you, as long as your anchored, you can be rocked all day long and even though it feels like you are moving you will not be moved out of your place.

The same holds true in the circumstances of life, even when it's calm we want our souls to be anchored to our spirit. That way we will not discreetly be pushed out of our place. And when someone or something comes to rock your world that anchored soul shall not be moved.

We all have times in our lives when situations rise up and endeavor to move our soul from the place of peace we are anchored to. People and circumstances will come to rock our world and no matter if it's a wind of sickness, a wave of depression, running aground due to lack or a big boat load of people causing strife and bitterness, we can stay anchored to our spirit. Once again this is done by expecting God to work all things out for our good. The positive hope activates our faith in what we know is true about God.

There is a story in Matthew chapter 7:24-27 (NKJV) of two builders.

> "Therefore whoever hears these sayings of Mine, **and does them,** I will liken him to a wise man who built his house on the rock: and the rain descended, the floods came, and the winds blew and beat on that house; and it did not fall, for it was founded on the rock. [26] "But everyone who hears these sayings of Mine, **and does not do them,** will be like a foolish man who built his house on the sand: [27] and the rain descended, the floods came, and the winds blew and beat on that house; and it fell. And great was its fall."

Notice that both these builders had the same storm and they both felt the forces of the wind, rain and floods. But only one was left standing.

Despite the pressures of the world and the emotions that try to pull us away, we can overcome every circumstance by following and doing God's Word.

> And we know that all things work together for good **to those who love God,** to those who are the called according to His purpose.
> **ROMANS 8:28 (NKJV)**

This is key to taking control of our souls.

God instructs us to be transformed by the renewing of our minds and to be doers of the word.

> Do not be conformed to this world but be **TRANSFORMED** by the renewing of your mind that you may prove what is that good, acceptable and perfect will of God.
> ROMANS 12:2 **(NKJV)**

Otherwise we will be moved out of the place we parked and can even run aground and be put in a dangerous situation.

Another analogy is setting the temperature in your home. If you want it to remain at 70 degrees you have to set the thermostat. The thermostat keeps the thermometer in line with where you want the temperature to be. The thermometer is **easily moved** if the climate changes. So no matter how cold or hot it gets and how often the thermometer is moved up or down. The thermostat will fight to uphold where it was set allowing a comfortable climate to remain.

SET THE THERMOSTAT OF YOUR MIND TO THE TRUTH OF GOD'S WORD AND NO MATTER WHAT THE CLIMATE YOU SHALL NEVER BE MOVED!

Staying rooted and grounded in the Word of God will protect us allowing the promise in Isaiah 54:17 (NKJV) to manifest...

> No weapons formed against you shall prosper
> and every tongue which rises against you in judgment
> you shall condemn.

The bottom line is the Word of God divides and it distinguishes between, letting you know if your soul is yielding to the five-sense realm or the Spirit. If we are not sure we can go to the Word of God that rightly divides. His Word is like a knife and it does surgery on your thought pattern and it will cut away to see what the root of the problem is.

> For the word of God is alive and powerful.
> It is sharper than the sharpest two-edged sword,
> cutting between soul and spirit,
> between joint and marrow.
> It exposes our innermost thoughts and desires.
> **HEBREWS 4:12 (NLT)**

God made it so easy for us as His Word and His Spirit will always agree so we will always know the ways to go.

> Your word is a lamp to guide my feet
> and a light for my path.
> **PSALM 119:105 (NLT)**

We cannot truly and intimately know God aside from His Word. Every problem, every weakness, every difficulty in our life can be solved as we know the mind and will of God. Knowing His mind and will come by knowing His Word.

There is however, so much in the five-sense realm grabbing for our souls in such a constant daily manner we must continually feed on His Word and fellowship with His Spirit.

We don't just want to know of God we want to KNOW God.

If I have a pitcher of water and I go out every day and get a little dirt in it but do not continue to pour in clean water it will eventually become dark and clouded. It is the same thing with our souls. The five-sense realm is consistently trying to pour dirt in your souls. What your mind thinks is a result of what you are feeding it.

> The truth is that, although of course we lead normal human lives, the battle we are fighting is on the spiritual level. The very weapons we use are not those of human warfare but powerful in God's warfare for the destruction of the enemy's strongholds. Our battle is to bring down every deceptive fantasy and every imposing defense that men erect against the true knowledge of God. We even fight to capture every thought until it acknowledges the authority of Christ.
> 2 CORINTHIANS 10:3-5 (PHILLIPS TRANSLATION)

A stronghold is something that takes a thought and captures your mind and then your thinking is in line with that thought pattern. This scripture is instructing us on how to take charge over that thought by capturing it and casting it out so it does not become a stronghold. The best way to change a thought is by speaking something out of your mouth.

You cannot fight a thought with another thought.

If you speak something out it will interrupt that pattern of thought.

To change your thought pattern, **speak** the truth of God's Word. It keeps our souls steady and even, throughout every storm life throws our way.

We must take control of the way we think and watch what we speak. Words are very powerful. Growing up I was taught… sticks and stones will break my bones but names will never harm me.

Unfortunately words spoken can do great harm.

Remember earlier we talked about how a train of thought will take you places. A wrong train of thought can take us on the road to derailment.

Derailment: the obstruction of a process by diverting it from its intended course.

Our adversary the devil would love to divert us from the intended course God has for our lives. He will try to do it anyway, with anyone he can.

> I have it all planned out—plans to take care of you,
> not abandon you, plans to give you
> the future you **hope** for.
> JEREMIAH: 29:11 (MSG)

Another translation says **plans to give you an expected end.**

The question then remains… What are you expecting?

We must get on the right train of thought to fulfill the destiny God has planned for us because what we are hoping for (expecting) plays a huge part in where we end up.

We are all looking for that good, pleasing and perfect life.

However, the customs of this world is to be lead by our emotions, this is why we need to be transformed.

Then we can be lead by the Holy Spirit. He will lead us to be overcomers of every negative circumstance that comes our way.

He will warn us of things to come and enable us to live out the plan that God has for our lives. Which is the most good, pleasing and perfect way to live on the earth.

Chapter 7

The Garden

HOW BEAUTIFUL AND SOOTHING is a well groomed garden. It has the ability to uplift your mood and bring a feeling of peace and comfort.

When we plant a garden we know that naturally whatever we plant is what we expect to harvest. Therefore, if we plant a certain type of seed that produces flowers we will eventually see those flowers growing in our garden. The same with vegetable seeds. If we plant tomato seeds we will get tomatoes.

Even though we do not plant weeds they usually grow in our gardens due to the natural elements. If we do not take measures to suppress the weeds or constantly pull them out they will eventually overtake the garden. Not only do they look bad but they take all the nutrients from the soil and eventually deprive the plants or vegetables we planted. This can cause them to do poorly and even die.

If we likened our minds to the natural garden we would see how important it is to plant the right seeds and keep pulling out the weeds.

Earlier we went over how our minds consist of our will and our emotions. If we allow seeds of fear to settle in and grow it will lead us to all sorts of unhealthy emotions.

Even if we purposely do not plant the negative seeds they will endeavor to creep in through many different avenues of the five-sense realm. Just like the weeds do in the natural garden.

Things we watch on TV or in movies will plant seeds in the garden of our minds. Conversations we have or listen to, articles or books we read, music we hear and sing to, will all plant seeds in the garden of our mind and create thought patterns.

Eventually these thought patterns will be spoken out of our mouths and become what we believe.

There must be a consistent effort to bringing our thoughts back to that positive expectancy of hope which will anchor our souls in faith for the good to come to pass.

It is so important to keep watch over the garden of our minds and consistently pull out the negative weeds as this will protect our spirit.

> Keep your heart with all diligence,
> for out of it spring the issues of life.
> **Proverbs 4:23 (NKJV)**

The heart this scripture is referring to is not our physical organ that beats, it is our soul...(our mind, will and emotions).

The emotional state of the heart affects the rest of a person. Guarding your heart will ensure you to live as an overcomer and be victorious over every circumstance that comes your way in life.

Being grateful for what you have no matter how much or how little is vital to success in this area.

Gratefulness will keep your heart satisfied and happy and the one thing that is needed is hearing and speaking God's Word. This will keep the garden of your soul clear of weeds, thorns and thistles.

3 John 2:2 (NKJV) says...

> I wish above all things that you prosper and be in
> health even as your soul prospers.

The condition of your soul will determine the wellness of your life.

> **Do not be anxious or worried about anything,**
> but in everything [every circumstance and situation]
> **by prayer** and petition **with thanksgiving,**
> continue to make your [specific] requests
> known to God.
> **PHILIPPIANS 4:6 (AMP)**

While there is so much more to learn and grow in the things of God, I believe that when you apply these powerful scriptures they will be a help to you.

If you are not already going to a church that teaches you these spiritual truths, then I encourage you to find one that does. This will help you walk in peace and do the will of the Father.

Be Blessed!

NANCY FRASER is an entrepreneur and has also been assisting her husband John in ministry since 2001. She has always been dedicated to helping people reach their goals. First as a fitness trainer for 14 years, and as a Realtor since 2003. In addition both her and her husband own a Christian-based childcare center.

In meeting a multitude of people over the years she has seen many struggle with fear and anxiety. This has created a passion in her heart to endeavor to help people be successful through truly knowing God who loves them unconditionally and by guiding them to implement His Word in their lives.

To contact please write to:
Nancy Fraser
P.O. Box 83
Amityville, NY 11701

Or email: AriseAnShine60.1@gmail.com

Made in United States
North Haven, CT
14 August 2022